i'm a chef & my kids want buttered noodles

a collection of recipes

heath schecter

photos by: heath schecter & garry rosenfeldt

copyright © 2017 heath schecter
all rights reserved.
isbn: 1978204507
isbn-13: 978-1978204508

for rachel, dylan and jules...you are my heart and soul, the reasons i do what i do, & why i get up every morning. you inspire, me every day, to be the best i can be, and always believe in me. i only hope to make you proud...and feed you good food.

i love you all so much...and stella too.

contents

acknowledgements	ix
introduction	x-xii
notes from heath	xiii

starters & small plates

beef tenderloin crostini	16
cured salmon w/ pumpernickel	18
grilled peaches, burrata & puffed pastry	20
johnnycakes w/ bacon & buttered bourbon maple syrup	22
potato pancakes	24
scallops w/ spicy bacon brussels	26
steamed pork dumplings	28

soups & salads

corn chowder w/ bacon	32
orange scented carrot soup	34
roasted red pepper soup	36
smoked tomato bisque	38
spring pea soup	40
cucumber & watermelon radish salad	42
smoked shrimp & quinoa salad	44
watermelon salad	46

contents

mains

blue corn tamales	50
bulgogi flat iron w/ kimchi fried rice	52
lauren's shrimp	54
"lox & bagels"	56
pastrami spiced salmon	58
sea bass w/ farro	60
shrimp & andouille jambalaya	62
the hangover helper	64

sous vide

about sous vide	68
asian marinated pork shanks	70
bbq pork belly	72
duck confit	73
elk roast	74
pig cheeks confit	75
harissa lamb chops	76
new potatoes	78
poached eggs	79
oxtail w/ cheesy grits	80
greek style pheasant	82
thai green curry tofu	84

contents

sweet things

bread pudding	88
vanilla latte crème brulee	90
flourless chocolate cake	92
lime granita	94
vanilla frozen custard	95

sides, sauces, seasonings & more

kimchi fried rice	98
"kraut"	99
spicy cucumbers	100
bloody mary sauce	101
brown butter	102
buttered bourbon maple syrup	103
crème anglaise	104
crème fraîche	105
fresh herb sauce	106
gochujang sauce	107
green curry paste	108
harissa paste	109
orange dessert sauce	110
soy dipping sauce	111

contents

sides, sauces, seasonings & more (cont'd)

bulgogi marinade	112
everything bagel spice	113
pastrami spice	113
sweet chai seasoning	113
bacon	114
beet cured salmon	116
granola	118
pasta dough	119
pickle it!	120
spicy korean spread	121
pizza dough	122
tomato jam	123
vinaigrettes	124
white wine vinaigrette	125
basil vinaigrette	125

index   128–133

one more...

buttered noodles	136

acknowledgements

again, to my wife & kids for their love and support. without them i'm just some shmuck that cooks.

my brother steve, for always encouraging me; and, lots of love, as well, to risa, lilly & molly.

dominic zumpano, you're an amazing chef & a great friend. thanks for letting me share the kitchen with you. i always have a blast, learn a lot, and you make me a better chef.

garry rosenfeldt, your awesome pictures led to the creation of this book.

nikki & paul for being the most amazing friends.

dan, russ, ravi, dave, & bubs (and their families), thank you for being "brothers" and always having my back.

barry sorkin, for your review of the book and being a long time friend.

my mom, for not being a very good cook, which led to my love of cooking.

my dad, who taught me how to grill.

my in-laws, mom & dad, becca, dan and nathan, for all your love and support, always.

beau mac and brian f, for being good friends, great chefs, and giving me a shot when i needed one.

the clan mcmanus, along with other friends & family that have encouraged me along the way.

chefs nate schomers & johnny carino for your friendship and inspiration.

my friends at *the gallery*

steven (& pam) handmaker, a life-long friend, for having me cook a party for you & your nice words for the book.

chefs: wilson, wolf, and [the late] humphrey of aci, i needed a new start doing something i loved. if it weren't for aci, i don't know where i'd be today.

all of you that support me on social media.

lastly, to anyone that has enjoyed my food.

intro

food: (noun): any nutritious substance that people eat or drink in order to maintain life and growth

cook·ing: (noun): the practice or skill of preparing food by combining, mixing, and heating ingredients

chef: (noun): a person who prepares food for people to eat

these words define the majority of who i am, personally and professionally. i am also a husband, son, brother, father and friend...and the people that refer to me as such, are who i love to cook for...usually.

i've been toying with the idea of writing a cookbook for about 15 years, before i ever became a professional chef, and now i finally have.

the title of this book came about over dinner with friends. we were joking about some of the fancy food i make, and how my daughter will rarely try any of it. my son, however, has taken a great interest in cooking, so he's game for anything. yet, having the title be: *i'm a chef, & one kid wants buttered noodles, but the other one is all good,* just didn't sound right.

this isn't one of those cookbooks that gets kids to eat vegetables. this book focuses on some of my "go-to" recipes, as well as ones i have created over the years. they aren't all "kid friendly", or at least when it comes to one of my kids. so, it just depends on you & your family. this is a book of recipes I have created based on my love for food, which goes way back...

it all started at an early age (because i was the chubby twin compared to my scrawny brother); and, in our house, my mom did most of the cooking. it was not very good, but we always had food on the table and didn't go hungry. my dad would handle anything grilled. so, it wasn't the bad cooking that made me love food, it was wanting better food, and that came from watching tv...which is where i first learned to cook.

every saturday afternoon, in the 80's, pbs aired cooking shows. i watched julia child, yan can cook, justin wilson, and the frugal gourmet. i also can't forget jacques pepin and sara moulton. this wasn't an option for me, it was a saturday afternoon ritual.

my first job, at 14 years old, was at the local hot dog stand. my brother and i did prep work and washed dishes. nothing makes more of an impression on a kid than scrubbing dishes with crusted-on chili that sat in a steam table all day.

intro

we worked there throughout high school, moved up to preparing food for the customers, and working the grill. this is where i first learned about "being in the weeds".

in high school, my best friend dave was also into cooking. we took a class called "chefs", and we would cook together to impress our girlfriends. in college, i continued to work in restaurants; however, my family never saw this as a career. so, i received a bachelor's degree in architecture from the university of wisconsin—milwaukee, worked in that field for 10 years, and hated every minute of it. i would continue to work in restaurants and bars on weekends because i loved the business; and, i still had a love for cooking.

i would always cook fancy meals for myself, friends, family and eventually the woman that stole my heart, my wife. before i even became a professional chef, my wife referred to me as "her chef", and at our wedding, she vowed to "never, ever, ever...cook".

after meeting my wife, we moved to arizona, got married, started our family, and then, after our second child, the recession hit. being in the building industry was not what anyone wanted to be in during this time, because everyone lost their jobs. i had a wife, 2 kids, a dog, a mortgage, and couldn't find a job at all. this was a really low time in my life; but, like the phoenix I rose up (see what i did there). i started a new life, and was on the path to finally doing what i love to do...cook. i registered at arizona culinary institute (aci), not because i didn't know how to cook, but because i wanted to make sure i was doing it correctly. also, it didn't' matter how many years of experience i had in restaurants, nobody was hiring some guy that spent the last 10 years working as an architect.

besides marrying my wife, attending aci was the best decision i had ever made. aci gave me new opportunities. after a couple of weeks there, i was introduced to chef beau macmillan. i was helping one of my chef instructors at one of beau's "lunch & learn" events. this event led to working for beau. then after beau, i met chef brian fierstein, and he gave me a job working for him at the restaurant where he was the executive chef. i learned a lot from beau and brian; and, to this day, they are still good friends.

i look at being in the kitchen as an escape. it doesn't matter how many hours i am in there standing, prepping, and cooking....i love it.

intro

the hours are long and the job is hard, but again, it doesn't matter, because i'm happy doing it. if i am creating, i'm zoned in, and the time flies by. whether i'm helping my friend dom at his restaurant, cooking a private party, or just making dinner for my family or friends, i'm happiest in the kitchen.

chefs are a strange bunch, we take that beating and go back for more, because we love what we do. i truly enjoy meeting other chefs, being able to share that love for creating food, and learning from each other...there's a bond there amongst the craziness.

i wrote this book because i love being a chef, i love to create new dishes, and i love to share them with others. we live in a society of many cultures, and within those cultures are their specific cuisines. moreover, the more you delve into their different cuisines, you can find so many similarities to the foods you are accustomed to. there may be different spices and levels of heat; but, i believe it's food that brings people of different cultures together. in my house, when my wife and i are entertaining, we are always gathered in the kitchen. this could primarily be because i'm always cooking; but, i truly believe people feel more comfortable when gathered around food. also, having a drink in hand doesn't hurt either.

within this book i give you some basic recipes, primarily because i feel you have to start out there, and then you can enhance those recipes and take them to wherever your imagination takes you. i also give you some recipes where i have taken some comfort foods and turned them inside out and upside down. basically, taking the aspects/flavors of these comfort foods and creating a completely different dish.

some of the recipes are very easy to execute, and then there are some that require a bit more skill and/or special equipment. don't let that deter you; I honestly think you can do it.

lastly, i am just a chef that loves to cook and be creative with food. i want to thank you for buying my first cookbook. i hope you enjoy it, find some recipes you like, and have fun recreating them.

cheers,

heath

notes from heath

my recipes will just reference certain words, like oil, salt or butter; so, this will clarify what i am referring to just in case a specific ingredient isn't called out.

salt - Kosher Salt

oil - cooking oil: vegetable, canola, blended, coconut, olive oil (not extra virgin, that's for dressings and finishing a dish)

butter - unsalted butter

pepper - fresh ground black pepper

sugar—white granulated sugar

brown sugar—light brown sugar

egg(s) - large chicken eggs

potatoes— russet/baking potatoes

ingredients: your finished product will only be as good as the ingredients you're using. not all unsalted butter is the same, they have different fat contents, and the higher the fat, the richer the butter. there are some fake olive oils out there, just do your homework. when it comes to extra virgin olive oil, look for a specialty store, where you can sample different oils. check the descriptions for the flavor profiles. try a few, they don't all taste the same.

tools: having some good tools are essential, like a good knife, measuring cups & spoons, and pots & pans. there are other tools i use all the time, such as: a digital kitchen scale, stock pot, spatulas, squeeze bottles, ring molds, stand mixer, microplane, blender, immersion (stick) blender, food processor (and a mini, or smaller insert) and a spice grinder (or mortar & pestle). you may have some of these items, or not; but, i wanted to list them if you were curious.

i also wanted to add a list of abbreviations & a conversion breakdown so you can scale the recipes any way you'd like.

T - tablespoon   tsp - teaspoon   c - cup

pt - pint

qt - quart

oz - ounces

fl oz - fluid ounce

lb - pound

1 lb = 16 oz

2 T = 1 fl oz = 6 tsp

1 c = 8 fl oz = 16 T = 48 tsp

1 Gal = 128 fl oz = 4 qts = 8 pts = 16 c = 256 T = 768 tsp

starters & small plates

beef tenderloin crostini

makes about 24 pcs

this is a great little appetizer you can serve at room temperature. the nice thing about it, is that you can make most of the components a day or two ahead of time, and then put it all together the day you're serving it.

- 1 baguette, sliced 1/2" thick
- 1-2 lbs beef tenderloin
- 2-3 red onions, sliced
- Oil
- 1 lb goat cheese
- tomato jam (page 123)
- 2 c red wine vinegar
- salt & pepper

1. in a skillet on medium high heat, add 2 T oil. season beef with salt & pepper. place tenderloin in skillet, and cook about 5 min per side. remove from pan, and place on rack to cool.
2. Prepare tomato jam per recipe on page 123
3. in a tall sided pan, over medium heat, add 2 T oil. sauté onions until they start to soften. season with salt & pepper. cover with red wine vinegar, lower heat, and cook until almost all liquid has evaporated.
4. in a bowl, add goat cheese, season with salt & pepper. mix with a spoon until smooth. add a little oil to loosen up if needed.
5. preheat oven to 350°. place sliced baguette on a sheet tray and brush each slice with oil. season with salt & pepper. toast bread in oven about 5-8 min. remove and allow to cool
6. spread goat cheese onto each crostini, top with a slice of beef, a dollop of tomato jam and a little red onion. season with a little salt.

beet cured salmon with pumpernickel   serves 4

i came up with this after the "lox & bagels" dish (page 56). i wanted a different take on that dish, one that was cold, and would start the meal off nicely. needless to say, a larger portion makes a great lunch. *Due to the cured salmon & pickled onion, this dish requires prep a few days in advance.*

8 oz beet cured salmon (page 116)

1 c crème fraiche (page 105)

1 large yellow tomato

6 slices pumpernickel bread

Oil

1/2 red onion, pickled (page 120)

1/4 c capers, drained

fresh dill

everything bagel spice (page 113)

salt & pepper

1. preheat oven to 300°, and place slices of bread on a sheet tray. brush each slice with oil and coat with "everything bagel spice. bake 5- 10 minutes, until dried out and toasted, allow to cool

2. break up toast, and place in a food processor and pulse into bread crumbs.

3. in a skillet, on high heat, add oil to come up 1/4". pat capers dry, and fry, this will take about 20 seconds. remove capers to paper towels to drain.

4. cut 4 thick slices from tomato, season with salt & pepper. slice salmon, your knife should be angled to get 8 thin, wide slices.

5. season crème fraiche with 1 T fresh chopped dill, salt & pepper.

6. just off center of plate, place a dollop of crème fraiche, then swoosh with spoon. lay tomato slice, top with salmon. off to the side, create a line with pumpernickel crumbs. garnish with pickled onions, fried capers and dill. finish with a little sprinkle of salt

grilled peaches, burrata & puffed pastry   serves 4

i first made this when creating a birthday dinner for my wife. peaches were just in season and i wanted to find a way to utilize them in a little start to the meal.

- 1 peach
- 1/2 sheet puff pastry (store bought)
- honey
- salt & pepper
- 1 burrata
- extra virgin olive oil
- micro greens

1. cut an 'x' at the bottom of the peach. place in boiling water about 2 minutes, then place in an ice bath. peel skin, cut in half and remove pit.
2. cut puff pastry into 4 rectangular pieces, brush with oil, season with salt & pepper and bake according to directions on the box.
3. brush peach halves with oil, season with salt & pepper, and grill peaches (on both sides) either on a grill or using a grill pan. allow to cool, then dice peaches.
4. on each plate: place a piece of baked puff pastry and top with "torn" burrata. using a kitchen torch (or the broiler) torch the top of the burrata. add the diced grilled peaches, a drizzle of honey, extra virgin olive oil, a sprinkle of salt, and micro greens.

johnnycakes w/bacon & buttered bourbon maple syrup serves 4

there are two things i love, bacon & bourbon, and this puts both of those things together. johnnycakes are thought to be the original pancake, also known as hoecakes, made with cornmeal and are gluten free...besides delicious.

- 1 lb slab bacon (make your own, page 114)
- 1 T sugar
- 2 c boiling water
- 1 egg (beaten)
- buttered bourbon syrup (page 103)
- 2 c fine ground yellow cornmeal
- 1 1/2 tsp salt
- 1/2 c whole milk
- reserved bacon fat

1. preheat oven to 425°, slice bacon 1/4—1/2" thick, place on a rack (on a sheet pan) and cook to desired doneness, reserve the fat.
2. in a bowl, whisk together cornmeal, salt and sugar. stir in boiling water, mix until paste is formed. add beaten egg and stir in milk until you get the consistency of mashed potatoes (could be plus/minus the 1/2 c).
3. in a skillet, on medium heat, add 2 T reserved bacon fat. spoon 2 T of mix and spread to 2" diameter cakes. cook until golden brown, approximately 3-5 minutes, flip and cook other side
4. make the buttered bourbon maple syrup per page 103
5. layer 3 johnnycakes, top with bacon, and drizzle buttered bourbon maple syrup

potato pancakes (latkes)

makes 1 dozen

potato pancakes (latkes) are one of my favorite comfort foods; moreover, they're a great vehicle for toppings. traditionally, they're eaten with sour cream and/or apple sauce...i'm not traditional. i like a dollop of crème fraiche (page 105), cured salmon (page 116) & caviar. sometimes, some soft scrambled eggs w/bacon & fried shallots. maybe a little brisket & pickled shallot, or sautéed diced apples w/ brown sugar & cinnamon. try substituting the russet potatoes for sweet potatoes (without the onion).

- 1 lb russet potatoes
- 1 egg
- 1/4 c flour (or matzo meal)
- 1/2 medium onion, pureed
- 1/2 tsp salt (more for seasoning)
- vegetable oil for frying

1. peel potatoes and shred, either w/ box grater or in food processor. place shredded potatoes in a bowl of cold water for about 5 minutes. drain and place potatoes in a kitchen towel, squeeze out as much water as possible.
2. in a bowl, combine (drained) shredded potatoes, pureed onion, egg, salt and flour—mix thoroughly.
3. In a large skillet, heat 1/2 c oil to 375°
4. spoon heaping tablespoons of potato mixture into hot oil, press into pancake shape. do not crowd the pan, but can typically fit 5-6 pancakes depending of the size of your pan.
5. cook pancakes about 5 minutes, until bottoms are golden brown, flip and cook additional 5 minutes. remove to drain on sheet pan with rack. season with salt.
6. keep warm in a 250° oven until ready to serve. or, once cool, store in zip top bags, reheat at 350° about 10-15 min, or until heated through.

Scallops w/ spicy bacon brussels

serves 4

by now, you should know i love bacon...so, i'll continue to incorporate it in my dishes when i think it enhances the dish. this is one of those dishes, because it goes great with brussel sprouts, and it plays nicely off the sweetness of the scallops and brown butter.

- 12 sea scallops, side muscle removed
- 4 slices (thick cut) bacon, diced
- 2 radishes, sliced thin
- 2 T brown butter (page 102)
- 1 chili pepper, pickled (page 120)
- 1 lb brussel sprouts, sliced
- 1 blood orange
- 1 T sriracha
- 2 T oil
- salt & pepper

1. cut the end off the blood orange, lay on one cut side, and cut remaining peel & pith off, exposing the flesh. cut between the membranes, removing orange supremes.
2. in skillet, cook bacon until crisp, remove to drain, keep 2T of fat in the pan, add brussel sprouts, season w/ salt & pepper, cook about 4 minutes. add sriracha & bacon bits, toss to coat
3. In a large skillet, over med-high heat, add 2 T oil. Pat scallops dry, season with salt & pepper, place into hot pan.
4. (cont'd) allow scallops to brown (2-3 min), flip, add brown butter, and brown the other side. remove from heat.
5. on each plate: arrange brussels along 1 side of the plate and top with 3 scallops. garnish with sliced radishes, pickled pepper and blood orange supremes. spoon some of the brown butter from scallop pan over the scallops and season with a sprinkle of salt

steamed pork dumplings

makes 2 dozen

these are little time consuming to make, but definitely worth it. if you don't have a bamboo steamer, you can set up a lidded pot with a steamer basket.

- 1/2 lb ground pork
- 1/4 c thinly sliced green onion
- 3/4 T soy sauce
- 1 1/2 tsp rice vinegar
- 1 tsp chopped ginger
- 3/4 tsp sugar
- 1 egg white
- 24-30 shumai or wonton wrappers
- 1/2 c thinly sliced napa cabbage
- 2 T chopped cilantro
- 1 1/2 tsp chopped garlic
- 1 1/2 tsp cornstarch + more later
- 1 1/2 tsp sesame oil
- 1/4 tsp pepper
- Soy dipping sauce (page 111)

1. in a large bowl, add pork, cabbage, green onions, cilantro, soy sauce, garlic, rice vinegar, 1 1/2 tsp cornstarch, ginger, sesame oil, pepper and egg white. mix to incorporate.
2. Sprinkle a baking sheet with corn starch. Set a small bowl of water on your work surface.
3. Starting with 1 wrapper, place a heaping tsp of filling in the center. Using your finger (or a brush), moisten the edges of wrapper with water. Crimp wrapper up around filling, squeezing slightly,
3. (cont'd) bring wrapper together like a beggars purse. *if using square wrappers, moisten all 4 sides, and fold wrapper at the corners, creating 4 points.*
4. place finished dumplings on starch coated baking sheet, cover w/ plastic wrap, repeat with remaining wrappers. Steam immediately, or freeze and steam later.
5. line basket with cabbage leaves, place basket in pot (not to touch water), cover & heat on medium. once steaming, arrange dumplings, cover & steam about 5-7 min to cook pork.

soups & salads

corn chowder w/ bacon

makes about 2 quarts

bacon, corn, potatoes and a little spice...a perfect soup on a cold day.

- 1 lb bacon, diced
- 2 tsp chipotle, ground
- 1 qt chicken stock
- 1/4 c heavy cream
- salt & pepper
- 1 c onions, small dice
- 1 lb potatoes, peeled & diced
- 1 lb corn kernels
- 2 T butter

1. in a 4qt pot, on medium heat, cook bacon until crisp. remove bacon to drain. leave about 2 T bacon fat in pot, drain, strain & reserve the rest for another time.
2. add onions to pot, and cook until softened. season with salt & pepper. add chipotle powder, cook 1 minute. add potatoes and chicken stock, bring to a boil, then reduce to a simmer until potatoes are tender, turn off heat.
3. in a skillet, over medium heat, add 2 T bacon fat. add the corn and sauté until slightly caramelized.
4. add half the sautéed corn to the soup pot. puree soup with an immersion blender (or small batches in a blender) until smooth.
5. add remaining corn to the pureed soup and stir in heavy cream and butter. season soup with salt & pepper.
6. ladle soup into a bowl, garnish with crumbled bacon and enjoy.

orange scented carrot soup

makes about 1.5 quarts

this is a nice and healthy soup, you can even eat it cold. if you would like to make it vegetarian, substitute the chicken stock for vegetable stock.

- 1 1/2 lb carrots, sliced thin
- 4 tsp fresh orange zest, chopped
- 1/2 c white wine
- 2 c water
- salt & pepper
- 2 c onions, small dice
- 1 tsp ginger, minced
- 2 c chicken stock
- 2 T oil

1. in a 4qt pot, on medium heat, add oil. once shimmering, add onions and carrots, season with salt & pepper, cook until onions are softened.
2. add orange zest and ginger, continue to cook 2-3 minutes. then add white wine, cook until almost evaporated.
3. add vegetable stock and water, bring to a boil then lower heat simmer.
4. simmer until carrots are tender. you should be able to easily stick the tip of a knife into them. remove from heat.
5. in batches, puree the soup in a blender until completely smooth. return the soup to the pot and check your seasoning.
6. ladle soup into a bowl, garnish with fresh chives and a drizzle of olive oil.

roasted red pepper soup

makes about 2 quarts

if you like red bell peppers, you're going to love this soup.

- 8 red bell peppers
- 2 cloves garlic, minced
- 1/4 c tomato paste
- 1 T cumin, ground
- 1 T cornstarch
- salt & pepper

- 1 c onions, small dice
- 2 T butter
- 2 qt chicken stock
- 1 1/2 tsp coriander, ground
- 2 T fresh cilantro, chopped

1. Cut peppers in half, remove stems and seeds, and place on a sheet pan (skin side up) under the broiler for 15 minutes. Once completely charred, place in a bowl and cover with plastic wrap to steam. When cooled, remove the charred skin and chop.
2. in a 4qt pot, on medium heat, add butter and allow it to start bubbling. add onions and garlic, season with salt & pepper, cook until softened.
3. add cumin, coriander, tomato paste, and cook about 3 minutes
4. Add peppers and chicken stock, bring to a boil and then lower to a simmer.
5. in batches, puree the soup in a blender until completely smooth. return the soup to the pot and check your seasoning.
6. in a small bowl, mix corn starch with a little water to create a slurry. drizzle slurry into soup and let it thicken a bit.
7. ladle soup into a bowl, garnish with fresh cilantro and pinch of ground cumin.

smoked tomato bisque

makes about 2 quarts

i remember cold winter days, and sitting down to a cup of tomato soup & a grilled cheese sandwich. well, this is the grown up version of that soup.

- 6 T chopped garlic
- 1/2 c celery, diced
- 1/2 jalapeno, chopped & seeded
- 1 qt chicken stock
- 1/4 c white rice, uncooked
- 2 T oil
- 1 c red onion, sliced
- 6 roma tomatoes, halved
- 3 c tomato puree
- 1 T fresh lime/lemon juice
- 1 c heavy cream
- salt & pepper

1. if you have a smoker, great, if not, set up a charcoal grill with a "cold side" or gas grill w/ a smoker box. smoke tomatoes for 45-60 minutes.
2. in a 4qt pot, on medium heat, add oil, and get it hot. add onions, garlic, celery and jalapeno. season with salt & pepper, cook until softened.
3. add chicken stock, tomato puree bring to a simmer. add smoked tomatoes and rice, cook until rice is tender
4. in batches, puree the soup in a blender until completely smooth. strain soup through a fine mesh strainer, return the soup to the pot, stir in cream, add lemon/lime juice, and check seasoning.
5. ladle soup into a bowl and enjoy.

note: if you don't have a way to smoke the tomatoes, you don't have to. you can substitute the jalapeno for 2 tsp chipotle in adobo. this will add a little smokiness to the soup.

spring pea soup

makes about 2 quarts

fresh peas always remind me of spring. Sometimes it is hard to find them; so, frozen are the next best thing...just make sure to buy the best quality you can find.

- 3 c onions, chopped
- 1 qt vegetable stock
- 2 T oil
- 2 T fresh mint, sliced
- 20 oz peas (more for garnish)
- salt & pepper

1. in a 4qt pot, on medium heat, add oil, and get it hot. add onions and sauté until softened.
2. add vegetable stock and season with salt & pepper. bring to a boil, then lower heat to a simmer.
3. add peas & mint and cook an additional 3-5 minutes. remove from heat.
4. in batches, puree the soup in a blender until completely smooth, and then return the soup to the pot.
5. ladle soup into a bowl, garnish with a dollop of sour cream, crème fraiche, or plain greek yogurt along with some peas, chiffonade of mint, and a drizzle of a good extra virgin olive oil.

cucumber & watermelon radish salad   serves 4

ribbons of cucumber, thin sliced watermelon radish, black tear drop grapes and pickled peppers come together in a light salad that is sweet, tangy with a little spice. this recipe works best by using a mandoline.

- 3—4 persian/kirby cucumbers
- 12 black teardrop grapes, halved
- 2 T fresh lemon juice
- micro greens
- 1 watermelon radish
- 1 anaheim chili pepper
- 1/4 extra virgin olive oil
- aalt & pepper

1. slice chili pepper and pickle it (page 120).
2. using the mandoline, slice the cucumbers, the long way, creating ribbons.
3. peel the watermelon radish, and slice thin rounds using the mandoline. cut rounds in half to create half moons.
4. in a bowl, add lemon juice. then whisk in olive oil, season with salt & pepper to create the dressing.
5. in the dressing bowl, add cucumber ribbons, radish, halved grapes and pickled chilis. toss to coat.
6. to plate: arrange 1/4 of the mixture, season with a sprinkle of salt and garnish with micro greens.

smoked shrimp salad w/ quinoa

serves 4

i thought up this dish after discussing a different idea with my friend, chef dom. we were talking about whipped feta, it stuck with me, and this came out of it.

- 20 x-large shrimp (16-20/lb)
- 2 c mixed greens
- 1/2 c fresh herb sauce (page 106)
- 1-2 persian cucumbers
- 2 T fresh lemon juice
- 1 carrot, sliced on a bias
- 4 skewers, soaked
- oil
- 1/2 c quinoa
- white wine vinaigrette (page 125)
- 12 grape tomatoes, pickled
- 2 T plain greek yogurt
- 1 T fresh mint, sliced
- 1/2 c feta
- brine (5 c water, 1/4 c salt, 2 T sugar
- salt & pepper

1. place shelled, deveined shrimp in brine, refrigerate 1 hr. then place 5 shrimp on each skewer
2. set up a charcoal grill with a "cold side" to smoke, or gas grill w/ a smoker box.
3. make quinoa according to packaged instructions. once finished, mix with 2-3 T white wine vinaigrette.
4. peel tomatoes & pickle them (page 120)
5. in a food processor, combine feta, yogurt, lemon juice & 2 T oil. process until smooth. mix in mint, season with salt & pepper.
6. dress the greens with salt and 2 T vinaigrette.
6. using a mandoline, slice cucumbers into thick ribbons. roll the cucumbers and dress with vinaigrette, salt & pepper.
7. toss sliced carrot chips with oil, salt & pepper. place on a sheet tray in a 350° oven for about 5-7 minutes.
8. arrange skewers on cold side of grill, smoke for 5 min, then move over direct heat for 1 min/side.
9. on each plate: place 1/2 c greens, 1/4 c quinoa in front & top w/ carrot chips. place shrimp on greens & drizzle with herb sauce. add a couple rolled cucumbers, pickled tomatoes, a few dollops of whipped feta, & a sprinkle of salt

watermelon salad

serves 4

this is an awesome salad, full of different flavors, textures and temperatures. it's perfect on a warm summer's night.

- 1 sm seedless watermelon
- 6 mint leaves
- 6 yellow grape tomatoes, sliced
- extra virgin olive oil
- 2 T champaigne vinegar
- 4 T lime granita (page 94)
- 1/3 c queso fresco
- salt

1. make the lime granita
2. remove rind from watermelon, cut the green skin from the rind, cut 1/2 cup of 1/4" diced rind and pickle it (page 120).
3. cut 2—1" slices of watermelon. sprinkle champaigne vinegar on watermelon slices, place in vacuum seal bags, add 4 mint leaves and seal. refrigerate 30 minutes. remove watermelon from bag, dice into 1" cubes. reserve remaining watermelon for snacks.
4. slice remaining 2 mint leaves into thin ribbons (chiffonade). crumble queso fresco.
5. to plate: arrange cubed watermelon down the center of the plate. add slices of tomato, then top with pickled watermelon rind and queso fresco. sprinkle with salt and drizzle extra virgin olive oil. when ready to serve, add lime granita and mint.

mains

blue corn tamales w/ sweet potato

makes about 12

this dish literally popped into my head. i'm pretty sure it was in a dream, and i had to make it. i've made tamales before, but i wanted to do something vegetarian and colorful.

- 2 c blue corn masa
- 1 tsp baking powder
- 2/3 cup vegetable shortening
- 1 tsp ground cumin
- 12-15 corn husks
- salt & pepper

- 1 qt vegetable stock
- 1/2 tsp salt
- 2 sweet potatoes
- 1-2 tsp chipotle in adobo
- kitchen twine

1. in a mixer, beat shortening with 1 T of vegetable stock. in a bowl, combine blue masa, salt & baking powder, then add to shortening mixture. continue to mix, while slowly adding stock, until you achieve a spongy texture.
2. soak corn husks in hot water.
3. peel & dice sweet potatoes. boil until tender. puree chipotle in adobo, until smooth. drain & mash sweet potatoes, add cumin, 1-2 tsp of chipotle in adobo (to taste), and season with salt & pepper.
4. Spread 1/2 c of masa mixture [evenly] across the top 1/2—2/3 of
4. (cont'd) husk (leave space on the ends and at the top). add 1-2 T of sweet potato filling down the middle of tamale. bring 1 side of the husk over, as the masa covers the filling, and meets the other side, then roll tamale closed. fold up the bottom, and tie the tamale closed.
5. set up a steamer and stand the tamales up, the water should not touch the tamales. cover and steam about 1 hour.
6. unroll the tamale, and garnish with your favorite salsa, guacamole, sour cream, queso fresco, corn, whatever you like.

bulgogi flat iron w/ kimchi fried rice

serves 4

i really enjoy the flavors of different cultures. moreover, i tend to sway towards asian influences...and this is one of my favorites.

- 4—6oz portions, flat iron steak
- 1 1/2 c bulgogi marinade (page 112)
- 1/2 c gochujang sauce (page 107)
- salt & pepper
- Kimchi fried rice (page 98)
- 4 eggs
- 4 T oil

1. place steaks in a zip top bag with bulgogi marinade, and marinate in the fridge 6 hrs to overnight.
2. day of: make kimchi fried rice, gochujang sauce and allow steaks to come to room temperature.
3. in a skillet, over medium high heat, add 2 T oil. remove steaks from marinade, season with salt & pepper, place in skillet. cook 5-8 minutes per side (depending on thickness), flip and cook the same amount of time. the ideal internal temperature is 130-140°. remove steaks from skillet, allow to rest, then slice steaks into 3-5 slices.
4. in another skillet, over medium heat, add 2 T oil. add eggs, 1 at a time, and cook sunny-side up, leaving a runny yolk.
5. to plate, place 1/2—2/3 c of kimchi fried rice on plate, add the sliced steak on to the rice, then top the steak with the sunny-side up egg. spoon about 2 oz of gochujang sauce around the rice. finish the dish off with a sprinkle of salt.

lauren's shrimp

serves 2

i was cooking dinner for friends, garry & lauren, and i found out lauren didn't eat what i was cooking. i asked garry what she eats and he said "salad". so, i was determined to come up with something spectacular for her, and this was it.

- 1 lb jumbo shrimp
- 1/4 c celery leaves
- 1/2 c grape tomatoes, sliced
- 2 tsp honey
- 1—2 T white wine vinaigrette (page 125)
- 2-3 T extra virgin olive oil
- 1 lg sweet potato, peeled & diced
- 1 plum, small dice
- 2 T brown butter (page 102)
- micro-greens (garnish)
- oil
- salt & pepper

1. set oven to 425°. toss diced sweet potatoes with oil, season with salt & pepper, spread onto a parchment lined sheet tray, and bake 40 minutes (turning half way).
2. quick pickle diced plum (page 120).
3. once potatoes are finished: in a skillet, over medium heat, add brown butter. add potatoes, toss to coat in brown butter, add honey and sprinkle with salt...toss to coat.
4. season shrimp with salt & pepper. in a skillet over medium heat, add shrimp. cook 2-3 minutes, once opaque (and pink), flip and cook
4. (cont'd) 2-3 minutes on the other side.
5. in a bowl, add celery leaves and sliced tomatoes. season with salt, pepper, and white wine vinaigrette
6. to plate, place 1/2 the potatoes down the center of the plate. place 1/2 the shrimp next to the potatoes. sprinkle 1/2 the tomatoes & celery leaves on top of shrimp and potatoes, as well as about 1-2 T of pickled plums. finish dish with a drizzle of extra virgin olive oil, a sprinkle of salt and garnish with micro-greens.

"lox & bagels"

serves 4

as a kid, we would go to my grandparent's house on [most] sundays for brunch, and there was always lox & bagels...it's one of my favorite things. so, I decided take this comfort food and shake it up a bit.

- 4—6oz portions salmon, skinless
- 1 1/2 c water
- 1 c white corn grits
- 12 T butter
- 3 T shallot, sliced
- 2 T heavy cream
- salt & pepper
- everything bagel spice (page 113)
- 1 1/2 c whole milk
- 4 oz cream cheese
- 1/2 c diced tomato
- 1/4 c capers
- Oil

1. in a sauce pan on medium high heat, add milk & water, bring to a boil. reduce heat to low, add grits and whisk until grits cook and thicken. add 4T butter & cream cheese, season with salt. you might need to add a little more milk to loosen the grits when serving.

2. in a small skillet on high, add oil to come up 1/8". pat capers dry and fry, it takes about 30 seconds, remove to drain on paper towels

3. coat salmon with everything bagel spice. in a skillet on medium heat, add 2 T oil. once hot, add salmon and cook about 3 –4 minutes, then flip. cook 2 minutes, turn off heat & allow the

3. (cont'd) residual heat to finish cooking the salmon

4. in a sauce pan, over medium heat, add 2 T oil. once hot, add tomato and shallots, season with salt & pepper, cook until shallots are softened. add cream, reduce heat and slowly add remaining butter, 2 T at a time, while constantly moving pan around. this will create an emulsion, and a nice butter sauce. season again with salt & pepper

5. time to plate: place 1/2 c of grits on center of the plate, add the salmon on top of the grits. spoon tomato shallot butter sauce over the salmon, garnish with fried capers and a sprinkle of salt.

pastrami spiced salmon

serves 4

i came up with this dish while enjoying a rueben sandwich. another comfort food where i wanted to take these flavors and spin them into something totally different.

- 4—6oz portions salmon, skinless
- 1 c "kraut" (page 99)
- 1/4 c sour cream (crème fraiche page 105)
- 1 tsp prepared horseradish
- 1/2 tsp worcestershire sauce
- 4 T oil
- pastrami spice (page 113)
- 2 T shallots, finely chopped
- 1 T ketchup
- 1/4 tsp hot sauce
- 1/4 c vegetable (or chicken) stock
- salt & pepper

1. make russian jus: in a skillet over medium heat, add 2 T oil, add shallot and cook until softened. add ketchup, horseradish, hot sauce, worcestershire, vegetable stock, and cook until reduced by 1/3. remove from heat, stir in sour cream, and season with salt & pepper.
2. make the "kraut"
3. in a skillet, over medium heat, add 2 T oil. coat salmon with pastrami spice, then add salmon to pan, cook 4 minutes, then flip, cook an
3. (cont'd) additional 2 minutes and turn off the heat. the salmon will finish cooking via the residual heat of the pan.
4. time to plate: place 1/2—2/3 c kraut, top that with the salmon, and then spoon about 2 oz of russian jus around the dish.

sea bass w/farro

serves 4

crispy skin sea bass with a warm, hearty, salad of farro, golden beets, broccoli & dried cranberries, with a red pepper sauce.

- 4—6oz portions sea bass (skin on)
- 1/2 c golden beets, diced
- 1/4 c dried cranberries
- 2 red bell peppers
- 1 T shallots, chopped
- micro greens
- salt & pepper
- 1 c farro, dry
- 1/2 c broccoli, chopped
- 1 qt vegetable stock
- 1 1/2 tsp tomato paste
- 1 tsp garlic, minced
- oil

1. in a large pot, on medium heat, add 3 cups of vegetable stock and the farro. cook until tender, drain any extra liquid.
2. cut red peppers in half, remove seeds and place on a sheet pan, skin side up. place under the broiler until skins are blackened. remove and place in a bowl, cover with plastic wrap 5 minutes. peel skins and chop peppers.
3. in a skillet, on medium heat, add 2 T oil. add shallots & garlic, season with salt & pepper, and sauté until softened. add tomato paste, cook 2 minutes, add peppers & 1 c vegetable stock. season with salt & pepper. then puree in a blender.
4. in a skillet, on medium heat, add 2 T oil. season sea bass with salt & pepper and place in skillet skin side down. cook until skin is crispy, about 4 minutes, flip and cook an additional 4 minutes. turn off heat and let it sit in the pan.
5. in large pan, add 2 T oil, then add beets and broccoli, cook about 4 minutes. add dried cranberries and farro, mix to combine and season with salt & pepper.
6. to plate, spoon about 2 oz of red pepper sauce, place about 1/2 cup of farro "salad" on plate, then the sea bass. season with a sprinkle of salt, a drizzle of oil and top with micro greens.

shrimp & andouille jambalaya

serves 8

when i was in my 20s, my friend dave cooked at a cajun restaurant, it was the first time i had jambalaya & creole food. since then, i have visited new orleans and i love the cuisine. this led to recreating this dish at home...my son loves this dish.

- 1 lb slab bacon, diced
- 2 lbs x-large shrimp (deveined)
- 2 green bell peppers, diced
- 2-3 cloves garlic, minced
- 2—14.5 oz cans diced tomatoes
- 2 c long grain converted rice
- 1 tsp thyme, dry
- 2 T smoked paprika
- salt & pepper
- 2 lbs andouille sausage, sliced
- 1 large onion, diced
- 3 stalks celery, diced
- 1 bunch green onions, chopped
- 2 c chicken stock
- 2-3 bay leaves
- 1 tsp cayenne pepper
- hot sauce (to taste)

1. put a stock pot (or dutch oven) on high heat to get hot, then lower heat to medium, add bacon and andouille sausage. cook to render bacon fat (can take 10 min or more).
2. add onion, celery, green pepper, garlic, season with salt & pepper, and cook until onion is translucent.
3. add spices and rice, cook about 5 minutes to toast the rice.
4. add tomatoes & chicken stock. bring to a boil, then lower heat to simmer. cover for 15 minutes.
5. remove lid, add shrimp and green onions, season with salt & pepper, stir, and put cover back on to cook an additional 5 minutes
6. remove lid, turn off heat, fluff the rice, remove bay leaves and serve. check the seasoning, and add hot sauce to taste.

the hangover helper

serves 4

we have all had those mornings (afternoons) after a night of debauchery, where the only thing that will help are some eggs, toast, greasy bacon and a little hair of the dog. well this combines it all into one dish...and you don't have to be hungover to enjoy it.

- 1/2 lb slab bacon (page 114)
- 1/2 loaf brioche bread (or challah)
- 4 T butter
- salt & pepper
- 4 eggs
- 1-2 c bloody mary sauce (page 101)
- 1 T white distilled vinegar

1. set oven to 425°. slice bacon into 4 slices, place on a sheet tray w/ a rack, and bake 8-10 minutes, flip and continue an additional 8-10 minutes, or until desired doneness.
2. slice 4 1 1/2—2" slices. using a 2" circle cutter (or a glass), cut out a round from each slice.
3. make the bloody mary sauce
4. get a pot of water boiling, and crack eggs into separate bowls. once water is boiling, add vinegar. using a large spoon, stir the water, creating a vortex, then slowly add 1 egg at a time and cook about 2-3 minutes. remove with a slotted spoon.
5. in a bowl, melt butter. dip each side of bread into it. in a skillet on medium heat, add the bread rounds, season with salt & pepper, and toast.
6. plating: ladle about 2 oz of bloody mary sauce onto the center of the plate (or into a large, shallow bowl), place your toasted bread and then the poached egg on top of it. lay the thick slice of bacon next to it and season the dish with salt.

Note: try poaching the eggs via sous vide, recipe on page 79

sous vide

about sous vide

if you have never heard of sous vide, it is a french term that translates to "under vacuum". this is a cooking method where ingredients are vacuum sealed in food grade bags, and cooked in a water bath set to a consistent temperature over a set period of time.

i have always been intrigued by new cooking methods and the science behind them. in 2012, i was fortunate enough to be contracted to create new recipes using the sous vide method. in exchange for the recipes, i was given the sous vide equipment. since then, i have really embraced the use of sous vide in how i cook, and recipes i create.

i believe in cooking (some things) via sous vide. i think it helps with timing, and it allows you to cook tougher cuts of meat without over cooking them. this method is different than using a slow cooker or braising "low & slow". by cooking proteins at a lower temperature, over a longer period of time, the meat becomes very tender. the reason for this, is that any fat within the protein will render out slowly; moreover, the connective tissue breaks down and the tougher cuts of meat become tender. the caveat to this, is that the temperature you are cooking the meat at, will be the same temperature of the finished product. so, braising a roast at 275°, over 8 hours, you will end up with very tender, melt in your mouth, gray piece of meat. cooking sous vide changes this dynamic. by cooking sous vide, you can set the temperature range you want to cook at, let's say 140° (medium), over 16 hours, and achieve the same tenderness of the piece of meat you braised. however, that piece of meat will have a doneness of "medium" all the way throughout.

equipment used for cooking sous vide at home are available and relatively inexpensive. you can find a sous vide "sticks" online for $100. also useful for sous vide, are vacuum sealing machines, which you can find for around $50. besides being able to keep food fresher, longer; vacuum sealers help remove as much air as possible from the cooking bags, so they don't float in the water bath. if your bag floats, the food will not cook properly.

without going into a lot of detail, you can research cooking time and temperatures, and "how-to's" for all different types of proteins, vegetables, and deserts online.

if you're game, give this cooking method a try, I think you'll like it.

asian marinated pork shank tacos   serves 4

these shanks become super tender and just shred apart.

- 2-3# pork shanks
- 2 cloves garlic, minced
- 2 T mirin
- 3 T rice wine vinegar
- 1/4 c ketchup
- 2 T sesame oil
- corn tortillas
- 2 limes, quartered
- oil
- 1" piece of ginger, minced
- 1/2 c soy sauce
- 2 T sriracha
- 1 T chinese 5 spice
- 4 green onions, chopped
- spicy cucumbers (page 100)
- pickled red onion (page 120)
- cilantro
- salt & pepper

1. place shanks in a large vacuum bag. create marinade, by combining all remaining ingredients, pour into bag w/ shanks, vacuum seal bags (stop vacuum before liquid gets sucked into sealing area). refrigerate 4 hours to overnight.
2. set up sous vide water bath to 170°
3. remove bag from refrigerator, place into water bath, cook for 36 hours.
4. after 36 hours, remove bag from water bath. cut open bag and carefully pour liquid into a sauce pan. cook sauce over medium heat until it reduces by 1/2 and has a thicker consistency.
5. shred meat from shanks, add to reduced sauce to keep warm.
6. warm tortillas in a skillet w/ oil. make tacos by filling tortillas with pork, spicy cucumbers, pickled onion, and cilantro. serve with wedge of lime.

bbq pork belly

serves 2—4

this pork belly has a nice smoky flavor. cut it up, sear it off and serve on some sweet potato pancakes (page 24). you can also toss it with a bbq sauce for a little appetizer.

- 1-2 lb pork belly, skin removed
- 1 tsp granulated garlic
- 1 tsp chili powder
- 1 T brown sugar
- 1/2 tsp liquid smoke
- salt & pepper
- 1 tsp granulated onion
- 1/2 tsp ground cumin
- 1/4 tsp dry thyme
- 1 tsp smoked paprika
- 2 T oil

1. slice a diamond pattern across the top of the pork belly's fat cap.
2. create a spice blend combining all dry ingredients plus liquid smoke and salt & pepper. coat pork belly with rub.
3. set up sous vide water bath to 160°
4. place pork belly in a large vacuum bag and vacuum seal it.
5. place bag in water bath and cook for 24 hours. once finished, remove bag and place in an ice bath (ice & water) to cool. once cool, remove pork belly from bag, wrap in plastic wrap, and place between to sheet pans with canned food (or weights) to "press" the belly overnight in the fridge.
6. slice the belly and crisp up in a skillet over medium heat with 2 T of oil. be careful, the fat will splatter.

duck confit

serves 2—4

to confit means to cook slowly in fat. making duck confit sous vide is really easy, and you don't have to worry about staying home with the oven on. you can find rendered duck fat through a butcher or order it online.

- 2 duck quarters (leg & thigh)
- salt & pepper
- 2 c rendered duck fat

1. season duck quarters with salt & pepper, wrap and refrigerate overnight
2. set up sous vide water bath to 180°
3. rinse duck quarters and then pat dry with paper towels. place in large vacuum seal bags with rendered duck fat and vacuum seal.
4. place in water bath and cook for 8 hours.
5. allow duck to cool, remove quarters from bag(s) and shred the meat.
6. reserve the fat, you can freeze it to use again to make more, or to cook potatoes in.

elk roast

serves 4

this was one of the recipes i created when contracted through a sous vide company. if you like game meat, here's a good one...if not, substitute the elk for an eye round roast or bone-in chuck roast.

- 2 lb bone-in elk roast
- 3 sprigs fresh thyme
- 2 bay leaves
- 3 cloves garlic (1 minced)
- 1 1/2 tsp cocoa powder
- 1/4 c beef stock
- 2 T oil
- 2-3 parsley stems
- 1 sprig fresh rosemary
- 1 1/2 tsp oregano (dry)
- 1 T smoked paprika
- 2 T dry red wine
- 1 T shallot, small diced
- salt & pepper

1. mix oregano, cocoa powder, smoked paprika to create a rub. season roast with salt & pepper, then sprinkle with rub.
2. set up sous vide water bath to 130°
3. in a large vacuum seal bag, place the seasoned roast, 2 garlic cloves, parsley stems, thyme, rosemary, bay leaves, beef stock and vacuum seal (be careful to not get any liquid in the sealing area.
4. place in water bath and cook for 24 hours.
5. remove bag from water bath, remove roast and pat dry, reserving cooking liquid.
6. in a large skillet, over medium high heat, add 2 T oil. sear roast on all sides, remove and set aside to rest. add shallots & garlic and sauté until softened. deglaze skillet with red wine, and cook until almost evaporated. add up to 1 1/2 c of reserved liquid and reduce to a thickened sauce. season with salt & pepper.

pig cheeks confit

serves 4

i love bacon, which is just cured and smoked pork belly; however, i think the cheek is my favorite part of the pig.

1 lb pig cheeks, cleaned
4 sprigs fresh thyme
2 cloves garlic, smashed

2 c rendered bacon fat
1 bay leaf
salt & pepper

1. set up sous vide water bath to 160°
2. place in cheeks in large vacuum bag with thyme, bay leaf, garlic and bacon fat and vacuum seal.
3. place in water bath and cook for 16 hours (can cook up to 24 hrs).
4. remove bag from bath, drain and reserve fat.
5. in a skillet, add 2 T of reserved fat. pat cheeks dry, season with salt & pepper and sear all sides of the cheeks.
6. shred the cheeks and toss with 1 T of reserved liquid, check seasoning.
7. the shredded meat goes great on top of potato pancakes (page 24) with a sunny side up or poached egg (page 79) on top.

harissa lamb chops w/ couscous   serves 2

harissa is an african spice blend, it's a little spicy and has a lot of flavor. it goes great with lamb, and many other items.

- 1 rack of lamb, frenched
- 1/4 c onion, small dice
- 2 T carrots, small dice
- 1 cloves garlic (1 minced)
- 1 c chicken stock
- 4 T oil

- 1/4 c harissa paste (page 109)
- 2 T celery, small dice
- 1 T shallot, small dice
- 1/2 c couscous
- 2 T butter
- salt & pepper

1. cut rack of lamb in half, coat with harissa paste. place halved racks in vacuum bags and vacuum seal.
2. set up sous vide water bath to 128°, place bag(s) in water bath and cook 2hrs (4 max)
3. in a sauce pan, over medium heat, add 2 T oil, and sauté onion, celery & carrots, season with salt & pepper. add couscous and cook about 2 minutes to toast the couscous. remove from heat
4. in a separate pan, bring chicken stock to a boil. Pour over couscous, cover, and let sit for 5 minutes.
5. remove lamb from water bath, remove racks from bag, pat dry, season with salt & pepper, and reserve cooking liquid.
6. in a skillet on medium high heat, add 2 T oil, sear lamb on all sides, then remove to rest. add shallots & garlic, sauté until soft, deglaze pan with reserved cooking liquid. reduce sauce, finish sauce with butter, season with salt & pepper.
7. To plate, cut racks into chops, serve over couscous, & spoon about 2 oz sauce over the chops.

new potatoes

serves 4

i love cooking new potatoes this way because i can have them cooked and ready for the meal. they're tender and infused with the flavor of the herbs and garlic. new potatoes, and fingerlings, vary in texture from baking potatoes, they're "creamier" due to a lower starch content. you can typically find a variety of new potatoes in your local grocery store. they come in red, yellow and blue.

- 1 lb new potatoes
- 1 sprig fresh rosemary
- 2 cloves garlic, lightly smashed
- salt & pepper
- 3 sprigs fresh time
- 1 bay leaf
- 1/4 c oil

1. rinse and dry potatoes.
2. set up sous vide water bath to 180°.
3. place potatoes, and rest of the ingredients, into a vacuum bag and vacuum seal it. place into water bath and cook 90 minutes (up to 2 hours)
4. remove from bath, cut a corner of the bag and drain the fat from the bag, reserving 2 T.
5. in a skillet, over medium high heat, add the 2 T of fat and the potatoes. sauté to crisp up the outside of the potato, season with salt & pepper.

note: try using rendered duck or bacon fat instead of oil.

poached eggs

This is a great way to make poached eggs and have them on hand since you can make them ahead of time and just heat up when needed.

eggs, in the shell

1. set up sous vide water bath to 140°
2. place shelled eggs into the water bath and cook for 45 minutes.
3. remove eggs
4. when ready to serve, crack egg open onto a slotted spoon over paper towels, then place egg where you are serving.
5. the eggs can be cooked a day or two prior to when you are planning to use them. if you want to do this, after step 3, place eggs directly into an ice bath to stop the cooking process, then store eggs in the fridge.
6. when you are ready to use them, place the eggs back into a 130° water bath for about 10 minutes to warm through, then follow step 4.

oxtail w/ cheesy grits

serves 4

if you've never had oxtail, i highly recommend it...it's delicious, especially over these cheesy grits. this is a 2 day event, and well worth it.

- 2-3 lbs oxtail, cleaned
- 1 sprig fresh rosemary
- 2 cloves garlic, lightly smashed
- 2 T dry red wine
- 6 T butter
- 1 c grits (yellow or white)
- 2 T oil
- 3 sprigs fresh time
- 1 bay leaf
- 1 T tomato paste
- 1 3/4 c beef stock
- 1 1/2 c water
- 1/2 c shredded cheddar cheese
- salt & pepper

1. set up sous vide water bath to 165°,
2. combine tomato paste, red wine and 1/4 c of beef stock. place oxtails in a large vacuum bag, along with marinade, fresh herbs and garlic. vacuum seal bag, do not get any liquid in sealing area. place bag in water bath and cook for 36 hours.
3. remove bag from bath, cut a corner of the bag and drain the liquid, reserving it for later. Pull meat from the bones, and remove extra fat.
4. in a large skillet on medium heat, add 2 T oil. add the oxtail meat, season with salt & pepper, and sear all sides.
5. add the reserved cooking liquid, and allow to reduce by half, creating a sauce. finish sauce by add 2 T butter and check the seasoning.
6. in a sauce pan, add water & 1 1/2 c beef stock and bring to a boil. whisk in the grits, continue to whisk until cooked and thick. add 4 T butter, cheddar cheese and season with salt & pepper. if too thick, you can add more stock.
7. in a bowl (or plate) serve a heaping 1/2 cup (or more) of the cheesy grits and ladle oxtail and sauce on top. finish with a sprinkle of salt.

greek style pheasant

serves 2

juicy pheasant, crispy skin seasoned with lemon & oregano, yum. you can substitute chicken into this recipe as well.

- 1 pheasant, split (backbone removed)
- 1 T fresh parsley, chopped
- 3 T fresh oregano, chopped (1 1/2 T dry)
- 1/2 c + 2 T white wine
- 1/2 c chicken stock
- salt & pepper
- 2 lemons
- 1 bay leaf
- 3 T garlic, minced
- 4-6 T butter
- 4 T oil

1. set up sous vide water bath to 160°.
2. slice 1 1/2 lemons into 8 slices
3. season each half of pheasant with 1 T garlic, 1 T oregano, salt & pepper. place each half in separate vacuum bags and add 4 lemon slices, 1 T white wine, 1 T oil then vacuum seal and place into water bath for 8 hours.
4. remove bag from bath, cut a corner of the bag and drain the liquid, reserving it for later.
5. in a large skillet on medium heat, add 2 T oil. pat the pheasant dry, season with salt & pepper, and place in skillet skin side down to brown skin
6. remove pheasant halves, place on sheet tray in 200° oven to keep warm.
7. lower heat of pan, and add 1 T garlic, sauté about 1-2 minutes. deglaze pan with 1/2 c white wine and reduce to almost evaporated. add chicken stock and reduce by 1/3. turn off heat, swirl in butter (2 T at a time), add 1 T oregano, juice of half lemon, and salt & pepper.
8. serve pheasant halves and spoon sauce over the top. this goes great with new potatoes or rice.

thai green curry tofu

serves 4

this is my favorite thai dish, and it's vegetarian. by starting this sous vide, you impart the flavors into the tofu.

- 1 lb firm tofu, diced
- 1 15oz can coconut milk
- 1/2 c red bell pepper, diced
- 1/2 c snap peas, trimmed
- 2 T brown sugar
- 2 T oil
- salt & pepper
- 2 T green curry paste (page 108)
- 1/2 c red onion, sliced
- 1/2 c japanese eggplant, sliced
- 1 T fish sauce
- 1-2 T fresh basil leaves (thai)
- 1 c jasmine rice

1. set up sous vide water bath to 185°.
2. in a bowl, combine coconut milk, fish sauce, brown sugar and green curry paste, mix to make marinade.
3. in a large vacuum bag, add diced tofu and marinade, vacuum seal, and place into water bath to cook 1 hour.
4. cook jasmine rice according to packaged directions.
5. 5 minutes before tofu is finished cooking, set up a large skillet over medium heat, add 2 T oil.
6. add red onion and bell pepper to skillet, sauté until slightly softened, about 3 minutes. add eggplant & snap peas, and sauté an additional 2 minutes. season with salt & pepper.
7. remove bag from water bath and add all contents to the skillet. cook to thicken sauce, about 5 minutes, check seasoning, then add in torn basil leaves.
8. to plate, serve 1/2 c cooked jasmine rice and spoon the green curry tofu over it, garnish with more basil

sweet things

bread pudding

makes 1 pan

call it baked french toast, bread soufflé, whatever you want...it's all just bread pudding. this is a basic recipe, and you can add any flavors, fruit, jams, etc. to make it your own. i like to add fresh (or frozen) blueberries, sometimes a 1/4 cup of bourbon (or more)... and yes, you can even add a 1/2 cup of pureed pumpkin and 2 T of pumpkin spice...if you're a pumpkin spicer

- 1 lb brioche (or challah)
- 1 1/2 c whole milk
- 2 3/4 c sugar
- 1 1/2 tsp vanilla extract
- 1 1/2 c heavy cream
- 6 eggs
- 1/2 lb butter
- 1 tsp salt

1. cube bread, if it is fresh, place cubed bread on to a sheet pan and into a 200° oven to dry it out.
2. in a sauce pan, on medium-low heat, add milk, cream and butter. heat until butter melts, watch to make sure it doesn't boil over.
3. whisk eggs and sugar until fully incorporated and pale yellow, then add vanilla.
4. slowly whisk warm cream mixture into eggs to temper them...if you add the warm mix into the eggs too fast, you'll scramble the eggs...not good!
5. pour custard over cubed bread, and allow it to soak about an hour. transfer to a coated 8 x 8 pan (or 8" round cake pan), cover with foil, and bake in 350° oven for 45 minutes. remove foil and bake an additional 15 minutes or until golden brown.
6. serve with frozen custard (page 95) or crème anglaise (page 104)

note: to make chocolate bread pudding, melt 4 oz of dark chocolate with the milk, cream and butter. i like to use 2 different dark chocolates, 2 oz of the darkest i can find, and 2 oz of 60% cacao.

vanilla latte crème brulee

serves 4

crème brulee is one of those classic desserts. there is something about cracking that caramelized sugar crust; moreover, the contrast in flavors and textures of the burnt sugar and creamy custard. this is one of my wife's favorite desserts...that doesn't contain chocolate.

- 2 c heavy cream
- 1/2 c sugar (more for finishing)
- 1 T espresso powder
- 1 vanilla bean, scraped
- 5 egg yolks
- pinch of salt

1. preheat oven to 275°
2. split vanilla bean down the middle, and using the back of the knife, scrape all the seeds. add bean, seeds, espresso powder, and cream to a sauce pan over medium-low heat. bring to a simmer.
3. whisk egg yolks and sugar until fully incorporated and pale yellow. add pinch of salt.
4. remove bean and slowly whisk warm cream mixture into egg & sugar mixture to temper them
5. pour custard mixture into 4 ramekins (or custard dishes). place ramekins in a baking dish, and pour boiling water into the dish until it comes half way up the ramekins.
6. place in the oven and bake 45 minutes or until custard is firm but still wiggles a bit (after 45 minutes, check every 5 minutes). remove ramekins, allow to cool and refrigerate at least 1 hour or overnight.
7. sprinkle an even coating of sugar over the top of the custard. use a torch to caramelize the sugar (or put under the broiler)

note: if you can't find vanilla beans, add 1 tsp vanilla extract after you temper cream into eggs.

to make chocolate crème brulee, after removing vanilla bean from warm cream, whisk in 4 oz dark chocolate, then continue with step 4.

flourless chocolate cake

makes 1 cake

if you love chocolate, you'll love this cake. it is a dense, rich, chocolate punch to the face.

- 8 oz dark chocolate, chopped
- 1 1/4 c sugar
- 1 c cocoa powder
- 1/4 c coffee liquor (optional)
- 1 c butter
- 6 eggs
- powdered sugar for garnish

1. preheat oven to 350°
2. in a double boiler, add chocolate and butter, heat until melted and smooth
3. remove from heat, and whisk in sugar. Once incorporated, whisk in 1 egg at a time.
4. sift in cocoa powder and mix until fully incorporated.
5. grease and line a 9" cake pan, fill with batter, bake in oven 25-30 minutes until cake has risen, the top has formed a crust and center is firm (use a cake tester).
6. remove from oven and place on rack to cool 10-15 minutes. then remove from pan and finish cooling.
7. if you do not wish to use the coffee liquor, skip to step 8. poke holes all over the top of the cake using a toothpick or cake tester. brush coffee liquor over the top of the cake, continue to brush liquor until all has soaked in.
8. once completely cooled, garnish with sifted powdered sugar.

i like to serve this with orange sauce (page 110), granola (page 118), & frozen vanilla custard (page 95)

lime granita

makes 4 cups

granitas are great, and you can make any flavor you like. they are wonderful as palette cleansers within a meal or as a dessert.

- 1 1/2 c fresh lime juice (12—14 limes)
- 1 tsp grated lime zest
- 3/4 c sugar
- 3 c water

1. in a sauce pan, on medium-high heat, combine water and sugar, bring to a boil
2. reduce heat and simmer 5 minutes
3. remove from heat and allow to cool
4. stir in lime juice and zest
5. pour into a shallow cake pan and freeze
6. stir every 30 minutes with a fork over 2-3 hours until slushy and granular

frozen vanilla custard

makes about 3 cups

frozen custard differs a bit from ice cream because it contains egg yolks. this is the basic recipe; however, you can do different flavors, by steeping ingredients during the heating of the milk. for example, you can steep black tea, or crushed pink peppercorns (I would suggest straining the mixture prior to tempering into the eggs). also, you can add mix-ins, such as fruit, jams, candies or caramel prior to freezing.

- 1 c whole milk
- 2 egg yolks
- 1 vanilla bean (1 tsp vanilla extract)
- 1 c heavy cream
- 1/3 c sugar

1. in a sauce pan, add milk and vanilla bean (split & seeds scraped). warm mixture to simmer, do not boil.
2. in a bowl, whisk egg yolks and sugar until thick and pale yellow.
3. remove vanilla bean from milk and slowly whisk 1/2 of the mixture into the eggs/sugar mix to temper the eggs
4. pour tempered mix back into the sauce pan and return pan to stove over medium-low heat. stirring constantly, the mixture will thicken. it is ready when it coats the back of a spoon, and when you run your finger across it, the line stays.
5. remove from heat and strain through a fine mesh strainer into a container sitting in an ice bath. once cool, add cream (also vanilla extract if not using a bean). cover with plastic wrap and refrigerate 4 hours to overnight.
6. add custard mixture to your ice cream maker and churn according to manufacturer's directions. remove, and place into a freezer safe container and freeze.

Sides, sauces, seasonings & more

kimchi fried rice

serves 6

fried rice is great, but adding kimchi makes it even better. the fermented, tangy and spicy flavors of kimchi really takes it to the next level.

- 2 cups cooked rice
- 1/4 c green onions, sliced
- 1 c peas
- 2 T sesame oil
- 1/2 c kimchi, sliced
- 1/4 c carrots, small dice
- 1/4 c bean sprouts
- 1 clove garlic, minced
- 1/2 c soy sauce
- salt & pepper

1. in a wok (or skillet), on medium heat, add 2 T sesame oil and beaten egg. scramble egg, then remove and set aside. add carrots and garlic, sauté about 3-5 minutes.
2. add rice, green onion and soy sauce, toss to mix. add egg back in, along with bean sprouts and cook about 3 minutes.
3. add peas and kimchi, continue to cook until everything is hot and fully incorporated. season with salt & pepper

"kraut"

serves 4

although this isn't a traditional sour kraut, the intentions behind this recipe is to incorporate some of the flavors of a traditional rueben sandwich.

- 1 1/2 lbs shredded cabbage
- 2 tsp caraway seeds
- 1/4 c mayo
- salt & pepper
- 2 T rendered bacon fat
- 2 T whole grain mustard
- 2 T red wine vinegar

1. in a large skillet, on medium heat, add rendered bacon fat, then add caraway seeds and cook 1 minute to release oils.
2. add cabbage and cook to soften.
3. add mustard, mayo, vinegar and season with salt & pepper. cook until all ingredients are incorporated. adjust seasoning as needed.

spicy cucumbers

makes about 2 cups

- 2 kirby (or persian) cucumbers
- 2 tsp gochugaru (or red pepper flakes)
- 1 tsp sesame seeds
- 1 1/2 tsp sugar
- 2 tsp rice vinegar
- 1 tsp sesame oil
- 2 T green onion, chopped
- salt

1. slice cucumbers 1/8" thick, set aside
2. in a bowl, combine remaining ingredients to make the marinade.
3. dip 1 slice of cucumber in marinade to taste. adjust salt & vinegar as needed
4. once satisfied, toss cucumbers in marinade to coat, refrigerate at least 1 hour.

bloody mary sauce

makes 1 1/2 cups

- 1 med shallot, diced
- 2 T worcestershire sauce
- 1 T prepared horseradish
- salt & pepper

- 1 c tomato sauce
- 2 tsp hot sauce
- 2 T oil
- 1 T vodka

1. in a sauce pan, on medium heat, add oil. add shallot and sauté until translucent.
2. add vodka (optional) and reduce until almost evaporated
3. add tomato sauce, worcestershire, horseradish, hot sauce and season with salt & pepper
4. adjust spice to your liking with more hot sauce, check seasoning.

brown butter

makes about 1 cup

1/2 lb butter (unsalted)

1. in a sauce pan, on medium-high heat, add butter
2. the butter will melt and the milk solids will separate out. when the solids separate, the butter can start to foam, keep an eye on it. when all the solids have separate out and it's a golden yellow color (and translucent)...this would be clarified butter (ghee)...we keep going for brown butter.
3. turning the clarified butter to brown butter happens rather quickly and you will want to use your sense of sight and smell from this point forward. if you don't hit the sweet spot, you go from brown butter to black butter.
4. as the milk solids begin to caramelize, the butter will foam, blow on the foam to check the color. when it starts to show browning on the sides and smells "nutty", get it off the heat, it's done.
5. as the milk solids begin to caramelize, the butter will foam, just kind of blow at the foam to check to color. when it starts to show browning on the sides and smells "nutty", get it off the heat, it's done.
6. strain thru a fine mesh strainer w/ a coffee filter into a heat resistant container.

note: if you end up with black butter, you can still make a sauce out of it.

in a separate pan, add 1/2 c of black butter, 2 T capers, juice of 1/2 lemon, and season with salt.

this goes great with a nice "meaty" fish, such as halibut or sea bass.

Buttered bourbon maple syrup

makes 1 3/4 cups

1 1/2 c maple syrup
1 T bourbon

4 T butter

1. in a sauce pan, on medium heat, add maple syrup and butter. bring to a boil

2. reduce heat, stir in bourbon. cook 1 min.

crème anglaise

makes about 3 cups

crème anglaise is a great sauce for desserts, it's similar to a frozen custard base prior to freezing.

- 1 c whole milk
- 1 vanilla bean
- 5 egg yolks

- 1 c heavy cream
- 1/2 c sugar
- pinch of salt

1. in a sauce pan, on medium-low heat, add milk, cream and vanilla bean (split, seeds scraped), and heat until simmering.
2. in a bowl, whisk egg yolks and sugar until thick and pale yellow.
3. remove vanilla bean and temper 1/2 the mixture into the eggs, then pour back into sauce pan.
4. heat, constantly stirring, until sauce thicken to coat the back of a spoon, and when you run a finger through, the line stays.
5. strain through a fine mesh strainer, into a heat resistant container within an ice bath to cool
6. once cool, refrigerate. this can be made up to 5 days in advance.

note: to make a citrus crème anglaise (like lemon), add 1 T of finely chopped citrus zest to strained crème anglaise.

if you do not have vanilla beans, and want to substitute vanilla extract, add 1 T after anglaise has been strained and is cooling.

crème fraîche

makes about 1 pint

this is a very basic recipe, and don't freak out, but you have to leave this out on your countertop for a day or 2...you'll be fine.

1 pint heavy cream (ultra-pasteurized)
4 T buttermilk

1. combine both ingredients in a lidded container (the plastic deli containers work great)
2. allow this to sit on your counter for 24 hours.
3. after 24 hours, check the consistency, it should look like pourable yogurt...if not, leave it out for 1 more day
4. once thick, refrigerate it, it will thicken even more.
5. season your crème fraîche with citrus zest, spices, etc.

fresh herb sauce

makes about 1 quart

this fresh herb sauce is great on anything from roasted vegetables, smoked shrimp to grilled meats.

- 2 c fresh parsley (flat leaf)
- 1/2 c fresh mint leaves
- 2 cloves garlic
- 1 c extra virgin olive oil
- 1 c fresh cilantro
- 1 cup green onion, chopped
- 2 lemons, juiced + zest of 1
- salt & pepper

1. in a blender, add parsley & cilantro (tender stems are ok), mint, green onion, garlic, lemon zest and lemon juice. blend to break everything down.
2. drizzle in olive oil
3. season with salt & pepper

note: if you prefer more "tang" you can add more lemon juice, or a little red wine vinegar.

gochujang sauce

makes about 3/4 cup

1/4 c gochujang paste
2 T sesame oil
1/4 c rice vinegar
2 tsp fresh ginger, minced
2 tsp honey

1/4 c sugar
1/2 c vegetable stock
1/4 c soy sauce
2 tsp garlic, minced
salt & pepper

1. in a blender, add all ingredients and blend until smooth
2. pour into a sauce pan, on medium heat, and reduce by 1/2.
3. season with salt & pepper

green curry paste

makes 1 1/2 cups

- 3 T minced lemongrass
- 1 medium shallot, diced
- 1" piece of ginger, minced
- 1/2 packed basil (thai)
- 1/2 tsp white pepper, ground
- 3 T fish sauce
- 2 T fresh lime juice
- 1 T olive oil
- 1-3 green thai chili peppers
- 4 cloves garlic, minced
- 1/2 c packed cilantro
- 1/2 tsp cumin, ground
- 1/2 tsp coriander, ground
- 1 tsp shrimp paste
- 1 tsp brown sugar

1. remove stems and seeds from chili peppers and dice (use 1-3 peppers depending on desired spice level)
2. in a food processor, add all ingredients and pulse to form a paste
3. add additional oil as needed to bring paste together
4. store in an airtight container in the fridge, or freeze it.

harissa paste

makes about 1/2 cup

10—12 dried chili peppers
1/2 tsp cumin seeds
1 tsp caraway seeds
1/2 tsp salt

3 cloves garlic, minced
1 tsp coriander seeds
1/4 tsp whole black peppercorns
2 T olive oil

1. remove stems and seeds from chili peppers and soak in hot water to rehydrate
2. in a sauté pan, on medium heat, add black peppercorns, cumin, coriander, caraway seeds. toast until fragrant.
3. remove from pan and grind to a powder with a mortar & pestle (or in a spice grinder)
4. add all ingredients to a food processor and pulse to form a paste
5. add a little water from the peppers as needed to help bring paste together
6. store in an airtight container in the fridge, or freeze it.

orange dessert sauce

makes about 1 cup

1 c fresh orange juice (2-3 oranges)
Zest of 1 orange, minced
1 T butter

1/2 orange marmalade
1/4 c sugar
pinch of salt

1. in a sauce pan, on medium heat, add orange juice, zest, marmalade and sugar
2. cook to reduce sauce by 1/2. sauce should be thick and syrupy, but pourable.
3. lower heat to a simmer, stir in butter, cook 2-3 minutes
4. allow to cool

soy dipping sauce

makes about 1 1/2 cups

1/3 c soy sauce
1/3 c sliced green onions
1 T sesame oil
1 T sambal olek

1/3 c rice vinegar
2 T mirin
1 tsp minced ginger

1. combine all ingredients and refrigerate 1 hour.

note: if you don't have sambal, you can substitute gochujang or sriracha.

bulgogi marinade

makes about 2 1/2 cups

- 1 asian pear (or an apple)
- 5 cloves garlic
- 1/4 c soy sauce
- 3 T honey
- 1/4 c green onion, chopped
- 1 small white onion, chopped
- 1" piece of ginger, peeled
- 3 T brown sugar
- 2 T mirin
- 1 T sesame oil

1. in a food processor, combine pear, onion, garlic and ginger
2. puree until smooth
3. empty mixture into a bowl, add soy sauce, brown sugar, honey, mirin, sesame oil and green onions.

everything bagel spice

makes about 1/3 cup

- 1 T poppy seeds
- 1 T dehydrated minced garlic
- 2 tsp coarse salt
- 1 T sesame seeds
- 1 T dehydrated minced onion

1. combine all ingredients and store in an airtight container

pastrami spice

makes about 3/4 cup

- 1/4 c coriander, ground
- 4 tsp sugar
- 2 tsp garlic powder
- 1/4 c black pepper, cracked
- 2 tsp paprika
- 2 T salt

1. combine all ingredients and store in an airtight container

sweet chai seasoning

makes about 3/4 cup

- 1 T cardamom, ground
- 2 T cinnamon, ground
- 2 T ginger, ground
- 3 T brown sugar
- 1 T allspice, ground
- 1 1/2 tsp clove, ground
- 1/4 tsp black pepper, ground

1. combine all ingredients and store in an airtight container

bacon

makes 2 1/2 - 3 1/2 lbs

i love bacon, it's plain & simple. it's easy to make your own, and you can slice it as thick as you want. you just need time and a smoker, or set up a charcoal grill to use as smoker. also, i do not use any nitrates in the cure (pink salt); so, once smoked, use the bacon within a week, or freeze it.

- 4—5 lbs pork belly, skin off
- 1/3 c brown sugar
- 1/4 c maple syrup
- 1/3 c salt
- 3 T cracked black pepper

1. rinse and pat dry pork belly
2. combine spices and maple syrup to create a rub, and completely cover the pork belly.
3. place in an extra large zip top bag, or a plastic container with a lid and refrigerate 5 days. flip over pork belly every day.
4. on 6th day, rinse and pat dry the pork belly. place the belly on a sheet tray w/ a rack and place it back in the fridge overnight, uncovered. this will help dry the outside of the belly, allowing the smoke to adhere better.
5. day 7, time to smoke. insert a probe thermometer, from the side of the belly going into the center. place the belly on the cool side of the grill (i smoke using a charcoal grill, with apple wood chunks), set your thermometer to 155°, close the lid and wait for internal temp to set off the alarm.
6. once the belly hits the right temperature, remove it from the grill to a sheet pan with a rack and allow it to cool, then slice it, or wrap it, but definitely cook some up.

beet cured salmon

makes 1 1/2 lbs

this is a basic beet cure for salmon, you can add any other spice blend you like to add different flavor profiles. if using whole spices, like peppercorns, fennel seeds, etc...you want to toast them in a pan to release their essential oils, then grind them up. lastly, you want to buy the best salmon you can, wild is better than farm raised.

- 2 lbs salmon fillet, skin on
- 1/2 c sugar
- 2 medium red beets, grated
- 1 c salt
- zest of 1 lemon
- 1 bunch of fresh dill, chopped

1. mix salt, sugar and lemon zest, this is your spice cure.
2. lay a piece of parchment on to a sheet pan, place salmon in the middle, skin side down
3. cover salmon with cure on both sides, press to help it adhere
4. mix grated beets and dill, then add this to both sides of salmon
5. fold parchment around fish, then wrap in plastic wrap
6. place another sheet tray on top of the salmon and then weigh it down with about 5 lbs of canned goods or a 5 lb weight. refrigerate for 2 days
7. remove salmon, wipe away beets and cure, do not rinse. slice salmon, holding your knife almost parallel to the filet, creating wide, very thin slices.

granola

makes about 3 cups

granola is one of those things you can eat right from the container, pour some milk over, top your yogurt, etc. i like to add it to salads and desserts for added crunch. you can customize your granola any way you like, just remember to always use "traditional rolled oats" not "instant" or "quick".

- 1 1/2 c rolled oats
- 1/2 c chopped pecans (or any nut)
- 1/2 c honey (or agave, maple syrup)
- 1 egg white
- 1/2 tsp—1 T Spices/seasoning
- 1/2 c puffed rice
- 1/2 c flax seeds
- 1/2 c vegetable oil
- salt
- 1/2 c dried fruit (optional)

1. set oven to 300°
2. lay a piece of parchment on to a sheet pan
3. in 1 bowl, mix dry ingredients and in a 2nd, mix the wet ingredients
4. add wet mixture to the dry and make sure everything is equally coated
5. seasoning: always season with a pinch of salt. next, determine how you want it to taste, sweet or savory, and go from there. start out by adding 1/2 tsp of seasoning, taste and add more as needed.
6. examples of seasonings are: vanilla extract, cinnamon, nutmeg, cardamom, allspice, thyme, cayenne, etc. also see sweet chai spice (page XX)
7. spread seasoned granola mix evenly on parchment lined sheet pan and place in oven. stir every 15 minutes until golden brown and dry, this can take up to 40-45 minutes.
8. once finished, mix in any dried fruit you want (1/2 c), spread evenly and allow to cool. then break it up and store in an airtight container.

pasta dough

this is a basic pasta dough. you can mix this by hand; but, the easiest way is to make it in a food processor. roll it out w/ a rolling pin, or invest in a pasta rolling machine. make all different types of noodles, raviolis, or agnolotti.

2 c all purpose flour
1 tsp salt
water

2 eggs
1 T olive oil

1. in a food processor, combine flour, salt, eggs, oil and 4 T water
2. process until mix forms a ball. if the dough is too dry, add more water (1 tsp at a time).
3. once a ball is formed, continue to process an additional 60 seconds to knead it.
4. remove the dough, cover it with a towel and let it rest at room temperature for an hour.
5. cut into 4 equal pieces, dust with flour, and roll out to desired thickness and cut to desired width. or, roll out using a pasta machine per manufacturer's instructions.
6. if making dough by hand, place flour on your work surface and create a well with your finger. add eggs, oil, salt and a little water to the center of the well. using a fork, start incorporating flour into the wet ingredients. once it's combined, knead the dough until it is pliable, then continue to follow step 4 & 5

pickle it!

makes 1 quart

pickling fruits and vegetables allows you to add an acidic touch to any dish. i like to do a quick pickle, because i'm impatient and want to be able to use my pickled ingredient within hours rather than days. this is a basic recipe for pickling liquid. you can add any spices and herbs you like, such as: peppercorns, allspice berries, mustard seeds, bay leaf, sliced onions, garlic cloves, chili peppers, dill or other herbs. also, the type of vinegar you use, will play a part in the overall flavor of what you are pickling.

- 2 c vinegar
- 1/2 c sugar
- 1 T each of any other addition
- 2 water
- 1/4 c salt

1. in a non-reactive sauce pan, add water, vinegar, salt, sugar and any other spice.
2. bring to a boil to dissolve salt and sugar, allow to slightly
3. place ingredients you are pickling in a heat resistant container that has a lid
5. pour pickling liquid over ingredient you are going to pickle. close the container and refrigerate a minimum of 30 minutes.

spicy korean spread

makes 1

this recipe came about after visiting my sister-in-law, brother-in-law and nephew [while they were living] in germany. i think everyday we snacked on pretzels & spundekäs, which is a cheese spread seasoned with paprika. so, i took that idea and gave it a korean spin. it's a great dip for pretzels and vegetables. i also like serving it with toasty bread or putting it on a

- 1 lb whipped cream cheese
- 1/4 c gochujang paste
- salt
- 1 T sesame oil
- 1/4 c green onions, chopped

1. in a bowl, combine cream cheese, gochujang, sesame oil and mix to combine
2. fold in green onions, season with salt

pizza dough

makes 1 large crust, or 2-4 smaller

i can eat pizza for every meal of the day. i can put bacon & eggs on it, or cured salmon & capers for breakfast. for lunch, some slices of prosciutto and top it with an arugula salad. dinner, well i'm a traditional guy, so sausage and/or pepperoni for me. i can even do a dessert with crème fraiche, fresh fruit, and a drizzle of honey. you are only limited by your imagination. needless to say, you need a good crust to use as your canvas; so, here's a simple one.

- 2 T sugar
- 1 T oil (more to coat bowl)
- 2 c bread flour
- 1 T salt
- 3/4 c warm water (110°)
- 1 tsp instant yeast

1. in the bowl of a stand mixer, using the paddle attachment, add the water, sugar and yeast. wait until yeast starts to foam, if it doesn't, the yeast is dead and you need to start over.
2. add flour, salt and olive oil then mix to combine. remove the paddle and attach the dough hook (spray it with non-stick spray) and knead the dough for about 10-15 minutes until smooth and very pliable.
5. grease a bowl with oil, add ball of dough, cover with a towel and place in a warm dry area to rise for 1 hour
6. once risen, roll out dough to desired shape, or cut and create smaller dough balls.

tomato jam

makes about 1 1/2 cups

- 1-14oz can diced tomatoes
- 2 T white wine vinegar
- 1 T garlic, minced
- 1 tsp basil, dry
- salt & pepper
- 2 T sugar
- 1/3 c onions, small dice
- 1/2 tsp thyme, dry
- 2 T oil

1. in a sauce pan, over medium heat, add oil, onion & garlic, and sauté until softened.
2. add tomatoes (w/ juice), basil, thyme, and season with salt & pepper. Cook for 5 minutes.
3. add white wine vinegar, continue to cook until almost all liquid has evaporated. check seasoning.
4. turn off heat, allow to cool, and store in a sealed container in the refrigerator.

vinaigrettes

vinaigrettes are an easy dressing to put together. all you need to remember is a simple ratio of 3 parts oil to 1 part acid; and, you can adjust this to your taste. if you like a more acidic tasting vinaigrette, just cut down on the amount of oil. now, there are different types of vinaigrettes, separating and non-separating, and these depend on the emulsion you create when combining the oil and vinegar. there are emulsifiers that are added to vinaigrettes that help the oil and vinegar come together, like mustard and egg yolk. food manufacturers use ingredients like xanthan gum to create, and hold, emulsions.

the flavors you can create for vinaigrettes are only limited to your imagination. the acid you use, such as the type of vinegar or citrus juice, as well as the type of oil, such as blended (50:50 vegetable and olive oil), extra virgin olive oil, or flavored oils. lastly, the seasonings you bring into the mix will help determine the flavor. you can add fresh herbs, citrus zest, soy sauce, chili peppers, miso, and even tahini.

i have included 2 simple recipes for vinaigrettes i use quite often. one is a simple vinaigrette that has a weak emulsion, it does separate; so, a simple shake prior to use will bring it back together. the second contains an egg yolk, which creates a stronger emulsion, and will keep it together. these 2 recipes will provide a good starting point, in which you can change them up and create all different kinds of flavor profiles.

i encourage you to play around with making vinaigrettes, they aren't just for salads, they enhance meats and vegetables as well.

white wine vinaigrette

makes about 1 1/4

- 1/4 c white wine vinegar
- 2 tsp sugar
- salt & pepper
- 1 1/2 tsp dijon mustard
- 1 c extra virgin olive oil

1. in a bowl, whisk together dijon, vinegar and sugar
2. slowly whisk in oil until combined
3. season with salt & pepper

basil vinaigrette

makes about 1 1/4

- 1/4 c champaigne vinegar
- 1 egg yolk
- 2 tsp honey
- 1 c blended oil
- 1 1/2 T dijon mustard
- 1 clove garlic
- 1 1/2 c basil leaves, packed
- salt & pepper

1. in a blender, combine vinegar, dijon, egg yolk and garlic, blend to combine.
2. put blender on medium-low setting and slowly drizzle in oil
3. add basil and honey, blend until smooth
4. season with salt & pepper

index

index

b

bacon, 114, *115*
- corn chowder w/ bacon, 32, *33*, 114
- johnnycakes w/ bacon & buttered bourbon maple syrup, 22, *23*, 114
- scallops w/ spicy bacon brussels, 26, *27*, 114
- shrimp & andouille jambalaya, 62, *63*, 114
- the hangover helper, 64, *65*, 114

baking powder
- blue corn tamale w/ sweet potato, 50, *51*

bean sprouts
- kimchi fried rice, 98

beef
- beef tenderloin crostini, 16, *17*
- bulgogi flat iron w/ kimchi fried rice, 52, *53*
- elk roast, 74
- oxtail w/ cheesy grits, 80, *81*

beets
- golden, sea bass w/ farro, 60, *61*
- red, beet cured salmon, 116, *117*

bread
- baguette
  - beef tenderloin crostini, 16, *17*
- brioche
  - bread pudding, 88, *89*
  - the hangover helper, 64, *65*

broccoli
- sea bass w/ farro, 60, *61*

brussel sprouts
- scallops w/ spicy bacon brussels, 26, *27*

butter
- bread pudding, 88, *89*
- brown butter, 102
- buttered noodles, 136, *137*
- buttered bourbon maple syrup, 103
- corn chowder w/ bacon, 32, *33*
- flourless chocolate cake, 92, *93*

greek style pheasant, 82, *83*
harissa lamb chops w/ couscous, 76, *77*
"lox & bagels", 56, *57*
orange dessert sauce, 110
oxtail w/ cheesy grits, 80, *81*
roasted red pepper soup, 36, *37*

c

cabbage
- "kraut", 99
- steamed pork dumplings, 28, *29*

capers
- cured salmon w/ pumpernickel, 18, *19*
- "lox & bagels", 56, *57*

carrot
- harissa lamb chops w/ couscous, 76, *77*
- kimchi fried rice, 98
- orange scented carrot soup, 34, *35*
- smoked shrimp salad w/ quinoa, 44, *45*

celery
- harissa lamb chops w/ couscous, 76, *77*
- lauren's shrimp, 54, *55*
- shrimp & andouille jambalaya, 62, *63*
- smoked tomato bisque, 38, *39*

cheese, *see dairy*

chocolate
- dark, flourless chocolate cake, 92, *93*

cocoa powder
- elk roast, 74
- flourless chocolate cake, 92, *93*

corn
- blue masa, blue corn tamale w/ sweet potato, 50, *51*
- corn chowder w/ bacon, 32, *33*
- grits, "lox & bagels", 56, *57*
- grits, oxtail w/ cheesy grits, 80, *81*
- husk, blue corn tamale w/ sweet potato, 50, *51*
- meal, johnnycakes w/ bacon & buttered bourbon maple syrup, 22, *23*

index

corn
    tortillas, asian marinated pork shank tacos, 70, *71*

cornstarch
    roasted red pepper soup, 36, *37*
    steamed pork dumplings, 28, *29*

coucous
    harissa lamb chops w/ couscous, 76, *77*

cranberries, dried
    sea bass w/ farro, 60, *61*

cucumber, persian/kirby
    cucumber & watermelon radish salad, 42, *43*
    smoked shrimp salad w/ quinoa, 44, *45*
    spicy cucumbers, 100

d

dairy
  cheese
    burrata, grilled peaches, burrata & puff pastry, 20, *21*
    cheddar, oxtail w/ cheesy grits, 80, *81*
    cream cheese, "lox & bagels", 56, *57*
    cream cheese, Korean spread, 121
    goat cheese, Beef tenderloin crostini, 16, *17*
    parmigiano-reggiano, buttered noodles, 136, *137*
    queso fresco, watermelon salad, 46, *47*

  cream
    bread pudding, 88, *89*
    corn chowder w/ bacon, 32, *33*
    frozen vanilla custard, 95
    "lox & bagels", 56, *57*
    smoked tomato bisque, 38, *39*
    vanilla latte crème brulee, 90, *91*

  milk
    bread pudding, 88, *89*
    buttermilk, crème fraiche, 105
    coconut, thai green curry tofu, 84, *85*

duck fat
    duck confit, 73

e

egg
    basil vinaigrette, 125
    bread pudding, 88, *89*
    bulgogi flat iron w/ kimchi fried rice, 52, *53*
    crème anglais, 104
    flourless chocolate cake, 92, *93*
    frozen vanilla custard, 95
    granola, 118
    pasta dough, 119
    poached, 79
    potato pancakes, 24, *25*
    steamed pork dumplings, 28, *29*
    the hangover helper, 64, *65*
    vanilla latte crème brulee, 90, *91*

espresso, powder
    vanilla latte crème brulee, 90, *91*

f

farro
    sea bass w/ farro, 60, *61*
    potato pancakes, 24, *25*

flour
    buttered noodles, 136, *137*
    pasta dough, 119
    pizza dough, 122

g

garlic
    asian marinated pork shank tacos, 70, *71*
    basil vinaigrette, 125
    bulgogi marinade, 112
    elk roast, 74
    fresh herb sauce, 106
    gochujang sauce, 107
    greek style pheasant, 82, *83*
    green curry paste, 108
    harissa lamb chops w/ couscous, 76, *77*
    kimchi fried rice, 98
    new potatoes, 78

index

garlic (cont'd)
    oxtail w/ cheesy grits, 80, *81*
    pig cheeks confit, 75
    roasted red pepper soup, 36, *37*
    sea bass w/ farro, 60, *61*
    shrimp & andouille jambalaya, 62, *63*
    smoked tomato bisque, 38, *39*
    steamed pork dumplings, 28, *29*
    tomato jam, 123

ginger
    asian marinated pork shank tacos, 70, *71*
    bulgogi marinade, 112
    gochujang sauce, 107
    green curry paste, 108
    orange scented carrot soup, 34, *35*
    soy dipping sauce, 111
    steamed pork dumplings, 28, *29*

granola, 118

grapes
    black teardrop, cucumber & watermelon radish salad, 42, *43*

greens, mixed
    smoked shrimp salad w/ quinoa, 44, *45*

h

herbs
  basil
    basil vinaigrette, 125
    tomato jam, 123
    green curry paste, 108
    thai green curry tofu, 84, *85*

  bay
    elk roast, 74
    greek style pheasant, 82, *83*
    new potatoes, 78
    oxtail w/ cheesy grits, 80, *81*
    pig cheeks confit, 75

cilantro
    asian marinated pork shank tacos, 70, *71*
    fresh herb sauce, 106
    green curry paste, 108
    roasted red pepper soup, 36, *37*
    steamed pork dumplings, 28, *29*

dill
    beet cured salmon, 116, *117*
    Cured salmon w/ pumpernickel, 18, *19*

mint
    fresh herb sauce, 106
    smoked shrimp salad w/ quinoa, 44, *45*
    spring pea soup, 40, *41*
    watermelon salad, 46, *47*

oregano
    elk roast, 74
    greek style pheasant, 82, *83*

parsley
    buttered noodles, 136, *137*
    elk roast, 74
    fresh herb sauce, 106
    greek style pheasant, 82, *83*

rosemary
    elk roast, 74
    new potatoes, 78
    oxtail w/ cheesy grits, 80, *81*

thyme
    shrimp & andouille jambalaya, 62, *63*
    bbq pork belly, 72
    tomato jam, 123
    elk roast, 74
    new potatoes, 78
    oxtail w/ cheesy grits, 80, *81*
    pig cheeks confit, 75

honey
    basil vinaigrette, 125
    bulgogi marinade, 112

index

honey (cont'd)
    gochujang sauce, 107
    granola, 118
    grilled peaches, burrata & puff pastry, 20, *21*
    lauren's shrimp, 54, *55*

horseradish
    bloody mary sauce, 101
    pastrami spiced salmon, 58, *59*

k

ketchup
    asian marinated pork shank tacos, 70, *71*
    pastrami spiced salmon, 58, *59*

kimchi
    kimchi fried rice, 98

l

lemon
    cucumber & watermelon radish salad, 42, *43*
    fresh herb sauce, 106
    greek style pheasant, 82, *83*
    smoked shrimp salad w/ quinoa, 44, *45*
    zest, beet cured salmon, 116, *117*

lemongrass
    green curry paste, 108

lime
    green curry paste, 108
    lime granita, 94
    smoked tomato bisque, 38, *39*

liquid smoke
    bbq pork belly, 72

liquor
    bourbon, buttered bourbon maple syrup, 103
    coffee, flourless chocolate cake, 92, *93*
    vodka, bloody mary sauce, 101

m

maple syrup
    bacon, 114, *115*
    buttered bourbon maple syrup, 103

marinade
    bulgogi marinade, 112

mirin
    asian marinated pork shank tacos, 70, *71*
    bulgogi marinade, 112
    soy dipping sauce, 111

mustard
    dijon, basil vinaigrette, 125
    dijon, white wine vinaigrette, 125
    whole grain, "kraut", 99

n

nuts, pecans
    granola, 118

o

oats, rolled
    granola, 118

onion
  green onion
    fresh herb sauce, 106
    kimchi fried rice, 98
    Korean spread, 121
    shrimp & andouille jambalaya, 62, *63*
    soy dipping sauce, 111
    spicy cucumbers, 100
    bulgogi marinade, 112
  red
    asian marinated pork shank tacos, 70, *71*
    beef tenderloin crostini, 16, *17*
    cured salmon w/ pumpernickel, 18, *19*
    smoked tomato bisque, 38, *39*
    thai green curry tofu, 84, *85*

index

onion (cont'd)
  shallot
    bloody mary sauce, 101
    elk roast, 74
    green curry paste, 108
    harissa lamb chops w/ couscous, 76, *77*
    pastrami spiced salmon, 58, *59*
    sea bass w/ farro, 60, *61*
  yellow/white
    spring pea soup, 40, *41*
    tomato jam, 123
    asian marinated pork shank tacos, 70, *71*
    orange scented carrot soup, 34, *35*
    roasted red pepper soup, 36, *37*
orange
  blood orange
    scallops w/ spicy bacon brussels, 26, *27*
  zest
    orange dessert sauce, 110
    orange scented carrot soup, 34, *35*

p

pasta dough, 119
  buttered noodles, 136, *137*
peaches
  grilled peaches, burrata & puff pastry, 20, *21*
pear, asian
  bulgogi marinade, 112
peas
  kimchi fried rice, 98
  spring pea soup, 40, *41*
  sugar snap, thai green curry tofu, 84, *85*
peppers
  bell
    green bell, shrimp & andouille jambalaya, 62, *63*
    red, thai green curry tofu, 84, *85*
    red pepper soup, 36, *37*
  chili
    anaheim, cucumber & watermelon radish salad, 42, *43*
    dried, harissa paste, 109
    chipotle in adobo, blue corn tamale w/ sweet potato, 50, *51*
    jalapeno, smoked tomato bisque, 38, *39*
    thai chili, green curry paste, 108
pheasant, greek style pheasant, 82, *83*
pickle it!, 120
pizza dough, 122
plum
  lauren's shrimp, 54, *55*
pork
  asian marinated pork shank tacos, 70, *71*
  bbq pork belly, 72
  pig cheeks confit, 75
  steamed pork dumplings, 28, *29*
potatoes
  new potatoes, 78
  potato pancakes, 24, *25*
puff pastry
  grilled peaches, burrata & puff pastry, 20, *21*
pumpernickel
  cured salmon w/ pumpernickel, 18, *19*

q

quinoa
  smoked shrimp salad w/ quinoa, 44, *45*

r

rice
  jasmine, thai green curry tofu, 84, *85*
  kimchi fried rice, 98
  puffed, granola, 118

index

s

salad
- cucumber & watermelon radish salad, 42, *43*
- smoked shrimp salad w/ quinoa, 44, *45*
- watermelon salad, 46, *47*

sauce
- bloody mary sauce, 101
- brown butter, 102
- buttered bourbon maple syrup, 103
- crème anglaise, 104
- crème fraiche, 105
- fish, green curry paste, 108
- fresh herb sauce, 106
- gochujang sauce, 107
- green curry paste, 108
- harissa paste, 109
- orange dessert sauce, 110
- soy dipping sauce, 111
- tomato jam, 123

seafood
- beet cured salmon, 116, *117*
- cured salmon w/ pumpernickel, 18, *19*
- lauren's shrimp, 54, *55*
- "lox & bagels", 56, *57*
- pastrami spiced salmon, 58, *59*
- scallops w/ spicy bacon brussels, 26, *27*
- sea bass w/ farro, 60, *61*
- shrimp & andouille jambalaya, 62, *63*
- shrimp paste, green curry paste, 108
- smoked shrimp salad w/ quinoa, 44, *45*

seasoning
- everything bagel spice, 113
- pastrami spice, 113
- sweet chai seasoning, 113

sides
- "kraut", 99
- kimchi fried rice, 98
- spicy cucumbers, 100

aoup
- corn chowder w/ bacon, 32, *33*
- orange scented carrot soup, 34, *35*
- roasted red pepper soup, 36, *37*
- smoked tomato bisque, 38, *39*
- spring pea soup, 40, *41*

sour cream
- pastrami spiced salmon, 58, *59*

sous vide, 68

t

tofu
- thai green curry tofu, 84, *85*

tomato jam, 123

v

vanilla
- frozen vanilla custard, 95

vinaigrettes, 124
- basil vinaigrette, 125
- white wine vinaigrette, 125

w

watermelon
- watermelon salad, 46, *47*

y

yeast
- pizza dough, 122

yogurt, greek
- smoked shrimp salad w/ quinoa, 44, *45*

one more...

buttered noodles

serves 2

this had to be the last recipe...

my daughter rarely eats anything i cook, and is stuck on buttered noodles. well, i think after all of the recipes in this book, we can do one hell of a buttered noodle dish that isn't boxed pasta and spray butter.

1/4 of pasta dough (page 119)

1 piece parmigiano—reggiano

flour

1/4 c brown butter (page 102)

2-3 T parsley, chopped

salt & pepper

1. sprinkle flour on to a work surface, and roll out pasta dough to about 1—1.5 mm thick (if using a pasta machine, check user manual for setting)
2. using a knife, or pizza roller, cut strips of pasta, as wide as you prefer. sprinkle with a little flour and allow pasta to dry about 5 minutes prior to cooking
3. fill a stock pot with water, season water with salt (should taste salty) and bring to a boil
4. add fresh pasta and cook until "al dente", typically about 3-5 minutes
5. in a skillet over medium heat, add brown butter and heat up. add fresh cooked pasta and toss to coat, season with salt & pepper
6. remove to 2 separate plates/bowls and shave cheese over the top and garnish with chopped parsley

chef heath schecter has worked in the restaurant industry, across various roles, for over 25 years. he has a bachelor's degree of architecture from the university of wisonsin-milwaukee, and attended culinary school at the arizona culinary institute located in scottsdale. he is a published author of recipes for a premier sous vide manufacturer and has worked along side celebrity chef, beau macmillan, at the sanctuary resort in paradise valley, az. heath is currently employed as a corporate executive chef for a food manufacturer. within this industry, he has developed and produced products such as sauces, spice blends, and ready-made deli salads. heath dedicates his free time to his family, and as a contributing chef at *the gallery* in lake forest, il, with his friend, james beard award nominee, chef dominic zumpano.

heath is also available for private chef services. you can visit his website at www.chefheath.com

Made in the USA
Lexington, KY
24 December 2017